Paper Boat

poems by

Lisa Conger

ISBN: 978-1-936769-17-9
Library of Congress Control Number: 2025916789

Cover Concept: Annica Eagle
Cover Design: Edmond Bruneau

FORWARD

It has always been a dream of mine to have a book of my own writing. It is a blessing and a privilege to share it with you, dear reader.

I believe that each of us is born with a creative spirit, and we can unleash that spirit to grow, create, and to heal.

Writing poetry has shed light on all that I am thinking and feeling. It has been a lifeboat as I navigate depression. And it has been a ladder that lifts my spirits. May the reading of these poems do the same for you.

According to John G. Stackhouse, Jr. *"Poetry condenses, compacts, crystallizes experience and insight. The best poetry is translucent, prismatic, kaleidoscopic: It lets light in and then splits it up, plays with it, in order to reveal something of the world previously unnoticed, or insufficiently celebrated, or inadequately mourned."*

I encourage you to let the pursuit of any creative endeavor – be it art, music, photography, cooking, drama, or writing, work its magic to both heal and enrich your life.

Don't know how to get started? Give yourself permission to begin. Read from an anthology of poetry to discover new poets, and relish again, old favorites. Take a class, keep a journal, take walks. Wake up to the life around you and the life within you. You might begin by taking a line from one of my poems and writing a response to it.

What have you got to lose?

Poetically yours,

Lisa Conger

TABLE OF CONTENTS

Paper Boat

Sometimes it feels as though
I have set out to sea
in a paper boat,
with nary a compass
nor star chart
to guide me.
But then I remember
we are each
and all at sea
in these waters of life –
riding the swells and troughs
of luck, determination, hard work.
And where are we going?
Is it in the stars
to circumnavigate the globe,
or to eddy deeper and deeper
in one place?
What I know is
my sails are filled with the winds of love,
and my anchor
a tether to gratitude.

Why I Write

Because the ink,
like Hansel & Gretel's breadcrumbs
lead me deep
into the forest of my heart.

Why I Don't Write

Because the ink,
like Hansel & Gretel's breadcrumbs
lead me deep
into the forest of my heart.

A Poem

A paper enchantment
performing
a certain magic
that can pierce the heart –
and soul –
to heal,
and make whole.

Attention

To pay attention
is the first calling
of the poet.
But, I often
find myself
adrift in my daydreaming –
my attention
dithering in the ether
of imagination's realm,
loosely meandering
far and wide.
But isn't my interior landscape
just as important
as reality's?
Inattention is
inner attention,
after all,
and all of it,
all of it,
kindling for the writer.

Some Wisdom

There are two ways of spreading light:
to be the candle, or the mirror that reflects it.
– Edith Wharton

Poets have much knowledge to share.
Even ancient poets offer timeless wisdom.
Rumi says, be a lamp, a lifeboat, or a ladder.
The problem is that folks
don't often listen to we poets –
after all, our heads are in the clouds,
and we are not known for our practicality.
But poets do pay attention to the world,
to both our inner and outer landscapes.
Our poems are both mirrors and windows,
and we poets are the candles
that can illuminate.

The Poet's Song

When I had no roof I made
wonder my roof. When I had
no walls, I made nature my home.

When I had no doorway,
I made truth my doorway.
When I had no light, I made
a lantern of my heart.

When I was thirsty
I drank in possibility,
when I was hungry
I feasted on awe.

When I had no companion
I made solitude my friend.
When I had no company
I opened my library of books.

When I had no playmate,
I smiled at the sea, waving to me.
When I had no lover,
I whispered to the moon,
my beloved confidant.

When I have no temple
my pen and paper become my prayer,
and all that I encounter,
holy.

Hidden Treasures

Reading a poem
is a process of discovery.
One looks for the hidden treasure within.
It could be the wording or phrasing,
the image,
or even the sound.
In poems that really work,
the hidden treasure
pierces the heart
in an instant of recognition and awe –
its meaning captivating and complete.
This is true in writing a poem, as well.
We poets seek the just right word,
or image, or line,
and pierce our own hearts
when we get it right.
That's where the light shines through.

As Writers, As Poets

As writers
we capture the words
we want to use
and put them in the cage
of form –
But they long not to be tamed –
to have their tongues tied,
to be tethered to sentences –
nor to be anchored by periods,
corralled into paragraphs,
or sent marching in columns.

As poets
we try to capture the words we want,
but do not bind or coerce.
We put our ears
to the beating hearts of words,
and listen to what they have to say –
the whispered yearnings, the little longings
that float from the throats of words.
We leave the cage door open –
and release them to try their wings
and take their own flight
right into our poem.

A Tanka on Writing

a long lost memory
comes to the forefront
in muted colors
by writing it –
it becomes vivid again.

Working Fire

The poets at the table
lean into their space
as pens and pencils
whisper across paper.
Chairs squeak,
gazes rest, unseeing
into space
before descending again
to the page.
Outside, autumn's glory
transforms trees
into pillars of flame.
Inside, here at this table,
a working fire of poetry
is ignited, is flaring –
spirits ablaze,
lives incandescently transformed.

Leaning Forward

Leaning forward, out of my life
I bend to needs, distractions, obligations,
but I dance to desires and longings.

And isn't this the way of the creative life?
Dancing to unheard music,
awakening to the dream's call?
How brave are you, you wonder,
as you pick up your pen,
or bring the brush to canvas?

What meaning can you make
that rivals the whisk of autumn leaves
twirling with their last gift of color,
or the drama of clouds stampeding
across the prairie of sky?
What movement stirs in you
like a chick whose pecking at her shell
releases her to this day's poem of being alive?

To witness, to transform, to write
that is what I must do
to make my life of meaning.

What if the Road?

What if the road
   is a typewriter ribbon
      which leads across the expansive
           paper white field —
a territory always ready to be explored?
       Poems like field poppies
         pop up
transforming the field to a meadow,
  while above,
    the stars of ideas glint and glow
     while the moon's gentle light
guides the heart
    on this inner journey
       of writing and exploration.
All it takes is courage
    to begin,
      and courage to persist.
 Know the journey will have twists
 and turns,
and the destination of print or publication
    will matter far less than
      the journey.

Snowflake & Star

"To appreciate the beauty of a snowflake it is
necessary to stand out in the cold,"
according to Aristotle.
And I say, to appreciate the beauty of a snowflake,
we must take the time to really look at one.
We must slow our need for action and be as quiet
in ourselves as the snowfall is over the landscape.
We must pay attention, like a poet.
Sir Francis Bacon says,
"Begin what you want to do now.
We are not living in eternity.
We have only this moment,
sparkling like a star in our hand –
and melting like a snowflake."
So true, so true.

Calendar Suite

Today

Morning rings all the doorbells,
evening turns on all the lamps.
Morning washes her face in dew,
evening showers with the meteors.
Morning arises, night falls.
Midnight turns over in bed.

Tomorrow

Tomorrow is a boomerang
flung forward in the calendar –
and always
it arrives back short –
today.

Yesterday

Yesterday suffers myopia
and fades slowly
like the letters
at the bottom
of the optician's chart
BLUR AND DIMINISH
UNTIL THEY
ARE GONE.

Someday

Someday sits in her fancy
dress – all spangled
and shimmery.
Her lips colored red,
ready to kiss.
You yearn for her,
always there is a secret longing –
but when someday arrives
now, in this moment,
your eyes are closed
or your back is turned.

Now

A niche in the great wall
of time –
a sheltered moment,
a shrine.

What's Next Now?

Is that you'll be
put on hold,
forced to listen
to some inane tune
over and over again
in an endless
telephone purgatory.
But, if we look at
what's next now
in terms of our own life,
what's next now
is a breath
followed by another
and so on,
until, there isn't
anymore.
So, don't put your life
on hold,
in an endless circuit
of waiting and wishing
wishing and waiting.
Take deep breaths
and live a rich life
of meaning and purpose
NOW.

Doing Time

My voice –
can you hear it whisper,
hear it shout? –
is trapped
in this prison cell
of a poem
doing time
in solitary confinement.
But if you read on
you allow sunlight
to splash through barred windows,
to puddle on the cement slab floor.
Smuggle in your attention
like a file in a cake,
and soon the cell door slides
past its latch
and I escape.
No probation.
No parole.
Just a free
verse.

Time Travel

The finitist
element of time travel
is the word.
Through words
we can travel across
continents and oceans,
through centuries,
through real and imaginary realms,
across the cosmos.
From earliest times,
humans have wanted
to make their mark.
On rock walls or in caves,
pictographs become symbols,
symbols become letters,
and letters become words,
and later, sentences.
So every time we read,
we are traveling through time.
Words have power.
They hide secrets,
convey emotions, and
truth tell.
One of the best gifts of literacy
is the ability to time travel.
Bon Voyage!

Good Fortune

Good fortune
is a gift
from gratitude.
And gratitude
is gracious –
it expands
in generosity,
and in vision.
The world,
seen through
the eyes of gratitude,
becomes even more
abundant and self-generative.
Good fortune
favors the contented,
and contentment comes
from simple gratitude.
You are lucky, indeed,
if you understand this
as early as possible
in your life.

Proverbial Wisdom

It may be better
to be safe than sorry,
but then,
your courage will not be exercised.
Be brave.

If you look before you leap,
keep your eyes wide open
for the world of black and white
may transform into prisms of color.
Be wise.

Do not kill two birds
with one stone,
but feed two birds
with one hand.
Be kind.

Christmas in Two Voices
(alternating stanzas)

Oh hell!
I touch my wallet reluctantly –
my fingers count out
the money slowly,
on my lips a curse
on all the cost
and fuss and bother.

> *Oh heart!*
> *I touch my chest*
> *with my palm*
> *and pat gently –*
> *A prayer of gratitude*
> *on my lips*
> *for all of life's abundance.*

Time shrinks
and patience narrows.

> *Being present*
> *time expands.*

The crunch of *"I wants"*
shout ever louder –
"Never enough!" leadens the heart.

> *The grace of peace*
> *sweetly whispers*
> *of love and simple kindness.*

The holiday lights' glitz & glare
insist I should be jolly,
but only fill
my frazzled heart with worry.

> *And a single candle's*
> *quiet radiance*
> *lights*
> *all the corners of my heart.*

Bah Humbug!
> *Joy to the World!*

Three Wise Snowman

The three wise snowmen,
bearing the gifts of
sparkling snowflakes,
glittering icicles,
and a precious fruitcake
wrapped up in a knitted
baby blanket,
were in a hurry
to reach the manger
before they and their gifts
melted completely.
Once that happened,
they would become
invisible, and disappear
from history.
All but the fruitcake,
which, as we know,
is still in circulation.

After Christmas Melancholy

A discarded Christmas tree
lies abandoned next to my neighbor's garbage can.
The plastic illuminated Santa is unplugged
and stowed unceremoniously on their small porch.
It is December 26th, and the spirit of the season
has flown from their home next to mine.

Meanwhile my two young adult daughters
banter and cheer in the kitchen,
make tea, nibble cookies, plan
their late night gatherings with old friends
home for this brief interlude
where they are not quite young deer –
both old enough now for wine and beer.
But when they leave the house
for icy streets I can't help but think
of them on wobbly legs,
learning to skate on this pond
called life –
etching their own destiny
in loop-de-loops & curlicues, and
the occasional bump to the bottom,
but always with that sparkle in their eyes
that illuminates their unique spirit.

I remember my Mother, gone now
the lifetime of my eldest.
I miss her now more than ever –
yearn for her kind and gentle touch –
knowing too, that I flew out her door
just as my daughters do now,
laughing, in the cold Christmas air.

Life is Short

Life is short,
but I don't keep it from my children,
they just don't believe me!
They are young enough
that the thought of mortality
belongs to everyone else,
not them.
Even when a contemporary dies
by suicide or accident,
they secretly believe
it won't happen to them.
Meanwhile, my guilty pleasures
are interrupted by the periodic flash
of recognition, that this will all
end too soon.
Should I be wasting time then
playing computer solitaire
or reading a trashy novel?
Ignoring kale in favor of ice cream?
And what of the perhaps morbid pleasure
I find in reading the obits each morning?
To each of those now dead,
their lives were just as real,
just as precious, and unique,
as mine.
And so I pledge through poetry
to find and celebrate beauty,
to seek the truth,
and to heal the wounds
I can. May I plumb the depths
of my own life,
whether it be long or short,
it's inevitable end
a calling to bloom
in every moment.
And at some point,
my children will have to
believe me.

How Hard it is to Be Outgrown

No more routing of monsters
under the bed
or in the darkened closet.
No nightlight needed now
nor hallway light left on, bedroom door ajar.
They go out for the evening
as I am just going to bed –
their evening starts just as mine ends.
Soon enough, our places are switched.
At dinner, my daughter points out
that I have spilled on my top
and tsk-tsks something about a bib –
she didn't really, but it surely felt like she had –
She quizzes me about my memory
and advises me about some thing or other
like I am an incompetent nincompoop
because I am afraid of
my new iPhone, and won't experiment.
Maybe I just need her assurance
that there are no monsters trapped inside my device
tapping at the screen to get out –
like the ghostly voice of Siri.

It Will All Come Out in the Wash

The white tee-shirt of peace,
the blue jeans of justice,
and the red bandanna of liberty
tumble together
in the wash of our world.
What is being laundered?

The tee-shirt is old and thin,
stained now with the sweat
of protestors bearing
heavy signs and banners.
The jeans are torn at the knees –
worn through from working
in the community garden,
and patched, many times
by calloused hands.
The bandana is faded now
from miles of street marches
protecting the head of a worker,
or wiping away tears from a tired face.
Can we ever come clean?

These colors are bleeding
in the hot water of war and political turmoil,
bleached by the media
through endless spin cycles
of permanent press,
the machine gone urgently berserk
(the control knobs click only to the right),
while the detergent of false cheer
clouds and dims these fabrics of hope.

These are the clothes
we take comfort and pride in –
their holes made holy
by our acts and by our allegiance to their ideals.
Though they be tattered rags,
we are called upon to wear them
again and again
until they are not simply garments
hung out to dry –
but prayer flags,
prayer flags of truth and transformation.

The Poet Looks at Her Own Work

and sighs.
So much of what she yearns
to write
is beyond words,
and sometimes they seem
to be hidden
behind layers of consciousness,
or tethered to a dream
insubstantial as smoke.
And yet,
that yearning
rises like a great whale
breaching the waves
in a great and lumbering grace
that breaks the surface
and manifests a holy wonder
which stops everything –
even breath –
in awe.
This messenger from the depths
can free my tears that mix with the salt
of the sea.
So, I begin again
ready to voyage on the ocean of blank pages
(as obsessed as Captain Ahab)
hoping once more for a sighting
and the slap of a grand tail
in greeting.

March Meditation

In the garden
everything is soaked.
Leaves drip
and soil loosened by moisture, gives.
Morning brings a greeting
from song birds lilting into damp air –
unable to contain their cheer
despite the soft pewter cloak of sky.
Tucked in a quiet corner
among the ivy and the day lilies,
whose fiery blooms seem far off,
a Buddha statue patiently smiles
awaiting the sun
to touch his round head.
At last, the sun breaks through –
ENLIGHTENMENT.

Incurable Joy

First, Kindness Clinics
popped up on every corner.
Inside each one kindness spread
like a virus –
infecting all within smiling radius.
Painless vaccinations
against snarkiness and sarcasm
were available for free to the teenagers,
with booster shots available to the older, more jaded.
Those who offered their arms without fuss
received comic bandaids and 2 oz. of dark chocolate.
Prescriptions for gardening, dog-walking,
and balloon-bouquet-giving were ushered in
as standard maintenance.
Whole therapeutic practices developed
around dancing, painting, and poem-making.
Instead of insurance claims, the only paperwork
involved tickets to art galleries, comedy shows, and concerts.
Library cards allowed 24-hour browsing
among stacks of books ceiling high.
Spirit Kitchens served signature chicken soup
and became more popular than any fast-food restaurant.
People lingered around tables laughing and conversing.
Then hospitals became havens for families working out issues
of anger, addiction and violence –
resorting to the resort-like atmosphere cultivated for curing:
soft lighting, lots of windows with garden views,
humble and wise staff, and quiet rooms where true sleep
was not disturbed or interrupted by poking or prodding.

Dogs, and particular cats made their rounds
offering their soft fur for petting -
the first protocol for treating high blood pressure.
Everyone had a voice in their own care,
and the time was taken to really listen to one another.
Patience referred to the qualities of staff,
not the status of the person.
Doctors whistled and nurses hummed –
music being medicine for the soul.
Joyfulness was infectious,
and the condition,
terminal.

Vessel

Sturdy and voluptuous,
this basket once belonged to my Mother.
She came under its spell in 1950's India
where she lived with my father and me
in a British compound.
Perhaps its beauty compensated some
for her loneliness.

It became a sewing basket
full of buttons, thread and thimble,
hidden under its domed lid.
Years later when my Mother's estate
was diffused, this basket full
of tangled thread and remnants,
was one item I chose to keep.

Why does it speak to me so?
Whispering its ordinary loveliness and fidelity
and holding its contents secure and private –
I think it embodies my Mother's struggle
with madness.
I fumble clumsily with needle and thread
and rarely spend time sewing,
But when I lift the faded lid
I am transported at once to my Mother's
love, and the life she stitched together.

A Sweetness

The breeze teases the skirts
of the petunias in their glazed pots.
A lone monarch butterfly meanders
on an inscrutable errand.
My mind wanders to these words:
Whatsoever things are lovely.
Think on these things
that I have framed on a wall
and to which I glance each morning.
Long ago my Mother sent me this verse –
never knowing that this very piece
would be a lovely thing
I think upon each day.
The bell of the wind chime's solo call
reminds me of her gentle spirit.
My heart now, a temple
in which her spirit-memory flickers
illuminating a path
as a candle in the dark.

Clay Owl

inspired by Susan Anderson

Bent over the pottery bench,
the creator pushes, pulls,
and shapes the clay.
She is fashioning an owl –
her spiritual totem.
She is grateful that the clay
is forgiving.
She can fold it in on itself
so it collapses,
and then form it once again.
She works steadily,
unaware of time,
humming as she works.
Finally satisfied with the form,
she whispers a little prayer
that the owl will impart
some sweet wisdom into her life.
Then, baptism by fire.

Cowbell

for Vern Hopkins

A sturdy cowbell,
gifted to me by
my favorite cowboy,
has accompanied me
through my days
as a workshop facilitator.
I used it to summon attention,
or when the writers –
especially the poets –
got excited and rowdy
and all tried to talk at once.
The inscription on the bell
once said,
"Cheney Rodeo Association,"
but it has worn away
from age and use.
Ironically, it got the most play
at the rodeo of writers,
wrangling their words
into order.

A Common-Law Marriage

for Rhea Giffin

The broom and the dustpan
are in a relationship together.
The dustpan, more appropriately called
the broom's companion,
is the broom's partner.
The broom tends to bristle easily
and get swept away into
far fetched notions and into
tight corners. And he has lofty
ambitions when he sweeps
cobwebs from the ceiling.
But the broom's companion
silently collects all the detritus that the broom
piles up, and patiently takes care of it.
Frankly, there is no substitute
for the broom's companion.
That flat piece of cardboard
is flimsy and meager and will not do.
No, they are in this together.
Where would each be without the other?

Call of the Wild, in Art

for Dallas

I can't precisely explain
my attraction to Native American art,
but there is something of the spiritual
in the abstract stylization of nature in the totems,
the fierce presences in the masks,
the motifs in the cloaks, and particularly
the whimsical, almost comical,
in the Inuit's birds and otters.
The intricately woven basketry,
the pottery vessels with
distinctive and recurring patterns
all express our efforts to connect to the divine
and to communicate stories or wisdom.
I once was gifted a kachina doll, a Corn Maiden,
by an albino Hopi Indian who befriended me
when I was working in Phoenix, Arizona.
Carved by his relative, I was honored,
and my profound thank you's
seemed entirely inadequate.
I wish I could say I have it now on display,
despite it's broken arm, but no.
It is tucked away in a box, wrapped in tissue,
and calling to me now.

Where I'm From

I am from my Mother's Jergen's lotion
and my Father's pipe tobacco.

I am from the house with green shutters
on a Southern California cliff,
and the little yellow one in Montana –
near The Sleeping Giant's lair.

I'm from the jacaranda tree
and the scarlet bougainvillea climbing the front porch,
and the purple lilac bush scenting
our yard under the Big Sky.

I am from the ink that ran in the veins
of my journalist parents.

I am from the blizzard Thanksgiving week of 1952,
christened, *"Rocky Mountain Gal"* by my great uncle.

I'm also from India's curries and bright saris
and an ayah who believed I was smart.

I'm from *"Rise & shine, it's daylight in the swamps!"*
called out by my father, a WWII Navy veteran,
and the bedtime stories improvised by my mother
as she tucked us in at night.

I'm from games of Scrabble and Monopoly
on weekend afternoons
and from Sunday comics read to us, and
after-church donuts.

I'm from a great grandfather in charge of a unit,
who captured John Wilkes Booth
after President Lincoln's assassination,
and was awarded a territorial judgeship in Montana,
before it became a state.

I am from a grandmother whose Dillon homestead
had a pasture with a horse named, *"44 More,"*
so her brother could brag he had 44 more in the pasture.

I'm from another grandmother who did morning chores
so her afternoons were free to paint watercolor landscapes.

I'm from breakfast picnics up Rimini Gulch,
and cozy time in the kitchen nook
of Aunt Dorothy & Uncle Gus.

I am from open-faced enchiladas with
homemade guacamole,
from exotic artichoke leaves dipped in butter,
and the strong black coffee I learned to like while camping.

I'm from expeditions to find Johnny-jump-ups,
Kinnikinick and Indian Paintbrush,
and I'm from a night mesmerized by the Northern Lights.

I am from a mother with a sensitive, artistic soul
who loved me dearly
and who died much too soon.

I am from a father distant
and unknowable.

I am from a sisterhood of two
who didn't always get along,
but love each other anyway.

I'm from my imaginary friend, *"Moody Conway,"*
short for Mohamed, my impish companion
who sometimes still dines at my table
when it's set for someone extra.

I am from the tongue of poetry
whispering, whispering,
"I am alive!"

Apples of Memory

Memories
are like apples,
plucked from a tree

Some are shiny,
ripe, with the sweetness
of love or friendship.

Others can be bitter,
best bitten into with
with care.

Some memories
are still vivid
even though they
are distant, shimmering,
from the top of the tree.

Still others
are faded, phantom,
impressionistic,
not quite clear.

Sadly, sometimes
memories get confused
and jumbled,
as if a clown
was juggling them ineptly.

The memory tree
continues to grow
as long as we do.
Feed it with your attention
and care.

Dog Ear

in memory of Susie

The black cocker spaniel mix
looks up to me
with imploring eyes.
Her left ear has folded over
and is inside out,
giving her a somewhat comical look.
I gently fold it back
before succumbing
to the great compulsion
to sink my face into her soft fur.
I murmur my sweet nothings of love
into this loyal and loving companion,
and I am happy.

Surprise!

While in grade school,
when my mother was in the hospital
for months, my grandmother came
to take care of us.
She looked stern, but was soft-hearted.
She read to us from the Little House series,
and told us about her life as a girl
on a Montana homestead.
She taught us how to make and sail
walnut boats in the sink.
She wore dark dresses, and sturdy shoes.
Fascinating to us, she kept her false teeth
in a glass beside her bed at night.
When we came home from school for lunch,
she made us sandwiches using
one slice of white bread, and one of whole wheat.
And she alternated soup offerings
between tomato and chicken noodle.
If we brought a sack lunch to school
in a brown paper bag,
it was always the same –
a sandwich wrapped in wax paper,
some carrots or raisins,
always an apple, and sometimes, a cookie.
One day I opened my lunch sack,
and discovered, along with the usual fare,
a ball of wadded tinfoil.
What's this? I carefully peeled it open
and found inside a little note
from my grandmother:
"Roses are red,
violets are blue,
Happy April Fool's Day to you!"

418 Via De La Paz

The Jacaranda tree
my father and I
planted together,
the house we lived in,
the elementary school
I attended,
along with the long walk
between them,
have gone in the devastating
Palisades Fire of 2025.
Gone is the backyard lemon tree,
the ice plant and the willow,
gone, too, the lanai and my hiding spot
I climbed to,
and all the geraniums my dog and rabbit
played beside.
Gone the green gate,
and the front porch,
the honeysuckle and oleander.
Everything burned
except memories,
now, thinner than smoke.

Just a Glimpse

A mid-February lull in the weather
leaves the large snowman melted
till all that is left is a pyramid of slush –
wire top hat askew, branch arms beseeching
in a gesture of a toddler asking to be lifted up.

On the asphalt nearby, five red rose petals
are scattered as if torn from their stem
in an emotional fit. They lie forlorn
in the grocery store parking lot,
where tire treads iron them obliviously.

A black and white dog in a rain parka
sits on a chair outside the coffee house
waiting on his master who has gone inside to order.
The dog looks at him over his shoulder,
his soft brown eyes wistful with longing and uncertainty.

The Japanese have a term
for *"beautiful sorrow,"* that describes
the beauty in sadness.
These things we seem only to notice
when loss vaults us into that spaciousness
of the vulnerable heart.

When we remember
what we have loved,
and lost, we glimpse
in these small moments,
a beautiful sorrow.

Letting Go

The petals of a bud
must let go and
release themselves
into blossom,
just as we humans
must release ourselves
from our own self-induced restraints –
letting go into self-forgiveness,
and awareness.
To begin, once again,
we must let go
of the held breath,
fears of ambiguity.
We must befriend uncertainty.

Dear Blank Page

Dear Blank Page,

Sorry I haven't written in awhile.

You look the same — unblemished by

the brush of a pencil,

the bruise of ink,

or the tattoo of script or doodle.

Have you missed me?

My thoughts — without writing them down —

are flimsy as smoke, wandering into the cosmos

and disappearing from memory.

It feels strange to mar your surface, and yet,

it also feels familiar.

Like I am writing my way home.

Yours truly,
Lisa Conger

A Gleaning

Once, on an archeological field trip
along the Sun River
we searched deep for evidence
of Blackfeet encampments –
desiring arrowheads or awls
or skinning tools beside
the Buffalo Jump.
My partner and I
found a pattern of stones –
a tipi ring,
and he, a graduate student,
disguised the coordinates
so no one else could locate this.
It soured me on anthropology
as a career, this deliberate
hiding of data, this selfish
act narrowing
instead of enlarging
understanding.
The good archeologists
are devout –
on their knees
magnetized by the possibility
of some minute find,
but I have to sing a different song
and find my worship
in poetry,
creating my own artifacts of words
to uncover my soul.

SWAK

Call me a naive romantic,
but I believe that the scientists are wrong.
Cosmologists believe the Universe began
with a Big Bang –
a violent explosion
that scattered everything
into fragments becoming
stars, planets, meteors, cosmic dust,
all that black matter that cannot be defined
as yet, and life. All life on earth.

No, I believe in fact, that it was
The Big Smooch
which created the love
that is the invisible force
that underlies the Universe.
We were kissed into existence
just as moonlight kisses ocean waves,
and sunlight kisses the top of your loved one's hair.
How else do you explain the existence of kindness
which softens the hard edges of experience
and caresses us with warmth and care?

It is no use arguing about
whose lips did such kissing in the beginning.
Our eyes are best closed
when kissed so deeply,
and it does not matter who.

The Beloved loves us
and in our loving of each other
and ourselves
we return and multiply
love's fragments.

And, as Emily Dickinson once wrote,
All I know of love is,
love is all there is.
I seal this poem
with a kiss –
SWAK!

Beneath Our Star

Life goes on –
the tiny ant trails up a mound,
the gray whale breeches into the air
where clouds lazily pasture
above the deep blue horizon.
Meanwhile,
the city streets are busy with people
coming and going,
opening doors or slamming them,
turning lamps on, or off.
Children's gleeful laughter fill
playgrounds with echoing joy
while teens check their techno gadgets
for the latest buzz
while bees drift in and out of
the throats of flowers
and opera singers practice
their scales
while fish mongers weigh
the tuna or the bass
while the bass player thrums
along with the saxophone
and couples are having sex
on beds or blankets spread
out beneath our star,
and babies are crying, mamas are cooing,
old men on benches are dreaming,
old women in kitchens are sighing,
all of us are living,
all of us are dying.
No moment the same,
each moment a gift.
Here, take this poem
and breath life into it,
for the tiny ant and great whale
know, as we keep forgetting,
we must live our life
in each moment
for that's all we have
beneath our star.

Midnight Snack

I drink in the beauty of a milk glass moon.
Do I have a telltale milk moustache –
a half circle of wonder, a crescent stamp –
above my lip? No, well then,
I'll just take another bite
out of this cookie moon
and feast until this phase is past,
or until
the moon rises whole again,
and I am full –
those stars
just crumbs scattered
on night's tablecloth.

Desire

Desire sings on the breath,
dances in the bones,
and plays the drum of the heartbeat
It is the energy of being alive.

Desire to shed winter's gray coat
shrugs the trees
into the light green wrap
of new leaves.

Desire sparks the flame of the bud
to ignite into blossom,
coaxed by the sun's
warm breath.

Desire journeys in the bee
from blossom to blossom
as pollen is tickled free
with the bee's light step.

Desire lilts from bird to bird
in a chorus of early morning greetings,
While desire sings a solo to the moon
with the coyote's howl.

It is the energy of being alive.
We are made up of desire –
for one more chance,
for one last dance,
for one last breath,
for one last prayer.

Wonder-Full

I am a Rocky Mountain
Big Sky gal
whose heart
also belongs to the sea.

Is it that spaciousness
of nature I seek
in order to mirror and expand
a spaciousness of heart?

As a poet,
I am always looking out windows,
or up at the clouds and stars.
I engage in a friendly
communion with that so much greater
than myself. I often
have conversations with the moon
and the aspen tree outside my door,
greeting them as friends. I wave
to the passing clouds, acquaintances
as flighty as butterflies, that I can
never hope to know intimately.

Yet, how is it that God or mountain,
sky, or stars squeeze to fit into the mind,
when it is the heart that makes the room?

How is it that the universe of space
can go on forever and yet begin in the pupil
of the eye?

How is that time seems to go by
in a blink?
Or is that a wink?

I wander
and
I wonder.

Grace

Born with the silver spoon
of moonlight in our mouths,
fed gold
on the tongue of dawn
each morning,
nourished every moment
on radiant air –
we feast.
Blessed with this bounty
we grow ever more full,
in gratitude.

If You Lived Here

If you lived here,
I'd know your name
like the grass knows
the bottom of my feet,
like the table knows
my elbow's gravity,
like the bathroom mirror
knows my gaze,
like my lips know
the whistle of my breath.
If you lived here
I'd begin to know you
like my heart wants to know
all the music of its chambers.

Come as You Are

God's hospitality
beckons through
the doorway of discovery
at the house of blessing.

Wipe your preconceived notions
on the mat of forgetting
and step lively into
the hall of love.
There are no stairs to climb,
no basement steps to fear.
You are finally and fully
here, in God's house.

You do not have to believe
a certain way
or act in a certain manner.
Just be who you really are
and you will see God's face
shining from the hall mirror.
Welcome.

Postcard Wisdom

"An artist is someone who finishes things."
- quote found on a postcard

An artist is someone who finishes things
and I know that Georgia O'Keeffe
gazing out her studio window
at the endless New Mexico horizon
was compelled
to paint
those bison skulls
and enlarged flowers
because she needed
to finish some conversation
within herself about

> bones and dust
> stamen and petal
> sky and cloud

in a symmetry of beautiful relationship.
But until we view her art
it remains unfinished,
for in looking at it
we each renew this conversation within ourselves,
and Beauty continues to ask interesting questions.

Elbow Room

Silence
allows
for a
spaciousness
which
gives
thought
elbow room
to turn
around.

To See Every Bird

To see every bird on earth
is not a dream I hold dear,
but to see,
really see
this one who has alighted here
on this pine bough
sinking and lifting now
as gravity adjusts itself;
this black bird
on Ponderosa limb
who looks askance at me,
who is it that he really sees?

I Have a Dream

I have a dream
that the Monarch butterfly
and the great Blue Whale,
the robin and the wolf,
the turtle and the giraffe
forgive us for our destructive,
thoughtless ways.

I have a dream that
the pansy and the Ponderosa,
the Aspen and the milkweed,
the apricot and the hollyhock
continue to offer us
shade and beauty –
sharing their abundance so generously.

I have a dream that
we all recognize
and appreciate
each being's infinitude and worth –
that this is the great lesson of life.
We need to be schooled
in the sacredness of all.
I have a dream.

Ask

Ask me
what the river sings
as its surface ice breaks free.

Ask me
about the embrace
of sunshine and snow,
melting slowly now.

Ask me
about the garden soil
softening in response
to the root's tentative grasping.

Ask me
what the birds declare
to the rising sun
with their choir of chirping song.

Ask me
why my heart lifts
on wings of joy
when the sun's warmth
begins its magic touch.

Ask me
why...

Personal Rites

My heart –
that temple bell
rings
a call to worship
to love's emissaries.

My eyes,
those wandering monks –
are washed with light
each morning
in absolution
before their call
to attend and witness.

My feet,
those paired pilgrims
find their path
step by step
through each day.

And my hands
open and close
before each task and tool,
missionaries
in the world.

The sabbath of sleep
soothes and renews,
and in the bell tower
the mind calls out
prayers of gratitude
and thanksgiving
for being alive.

Westward

A continent of grass
meets the eyes of pioneers
wagoning westward across the plains.
Wind chaps their lips
even as they murmur prayers
before the cathedral of sky.
Thin soles press against rock and stone
and eyes press toward the horizon,
searching, always searching.
The unknown has no boundary
save for the end of the familiar plough
in the calloused hand.
A small rag doll,
her china bisque face
chipped at the hairline
stares unblinking
at what was left behind,
as she gazes over the shoulder
of the child clutching her.
Their matching aprons and bonnets
are covered in dust.
As the child treads along,
her blue eyes tilt upward
to mirror the sky's bright blaze,
her small footsteps
are swallowed
in the grass
behind her.

The Invitation

I received a hand-delivered,
invitation to tea at *Mansfield Park*.
It did not take much *persuasion*
for me to RSVP a yes.
My heart was aflutter with excitement,
tinged a bit with dread.
Could I be a worthy conversation partner
to my companion's famous wit
and uncanny observations of society?
I would have to tuck my shyness
under my hat and come to my *senses* –
surely she would not hold my awkward
and inept *sensibilities* against me.
She *prided* herself on holding
no *prejudices* against those who were
genuine and sincere –
but woe to those fools she found to be
fussy and full of folderol,
twattling on about nothingness,
so negligent of significance.
I take a deep breath,
and with gloved hand,
knock on Miss J.A.'s door.

Poetic License

It is raining cats and dogs
and William Carlos Williams looks out
the farmhouse window,
to see it glaze the red wheelbarrow
beside the white chickens.

And Carl Sandburg
sees the hog on ice,
just before the fog comes
on little cat feet.

And e.e. cummings
is delighted
because now
the world is puddle wonderful
in just spring.

Soon Emily Dickinson will have
feathered her nest with hope
her words soaring
close to the rainbow.

Laguna Beach Divinity

At the holy altar of the beach
worshippers pray,
each in their own fashion.

Children, giddy with delight
call out to one another
expressing their natural souls.

Families bend and kneel in reverence
to tide pool and rock.
Others, like barefoot monks
walk their meditations
to the chant of the steadfast surf.

Vegetation, like a choir
sing out their colorful praises
to sun and balmy air.

The birds, lay leaders
to this congregation of life,
lead us in uplifted spirit
while the gentle wind brings
communion salt to our lips and noses,
here, at the holy altar of the beach.

Seasonal Haiku

Spring

front yard birch tree hosts
four fat robins
spring's candelabra

the new grass of spring
so very deeply verdant
it jabs my eyesight

the whispering wind
gossips among the green leaves
rumors and secrets

Summer

the red ladybug
clambers up the dying leaf
like a circus clown

summer heat sizzles
rising from the concrete walk
tender feet hopscotch

the beach ball escapes
children's reach as wind plays tag
with the incoming waves

Fall

fallen leaves skitter
in a wild whirlwind of dance
partnered by the wind

a flock of blackbirds
congregate on the front lawn
black feathered friars

late afternoon light
brings an amber ambiance
to envelope us

Winter

bare limbed trees reach out
to the star strewn sky above
clarity graces cold

a walk in the park
the only sound my footsteps
on the crunchy snow

fresh rains wash away
the mounds of dirty snow left
by tired snowplows

Alchemy

The row of ornamental grasses
bordering the parking lot
shimmer and tremble
in the pale gold of their dresses.
Like a chorus line of dancers,
they arch and bow
parry and turn
in a madcap promenade
choreographed by November's wind.
Stunned by the simplicity of their beauty
I pause and reflect on the poet's declaration,
nothing gold can stay,
and recognize in all things,
the alchemy of light.

Green, Green, My World is Green
for C.L. Crowell

Green is my favorite color:
the gold-green of new growth foliage
in early spring,
the blades of darker green
accompanying tulips and daffodils,
the deepening green of a spring lawn
emerging from winter's clutch,
the velvety moss green
abundant in the forests of the Northwest,
the still green of a mirrored pond,
the seeded bright green of a kiwi,
the softer gray-green of steamed artichoke,
the iron-rich green of spinach,
the piquant green of green onions for eating,
and the jazzy tune, *"Green Onion,"* –
chives or jives –
a palate of green for tongue or ear.
I see green and am happy.

Rain

Knots of pregnant clouds
hold back until the crack
of lightning and the call of thunder
insist its time. Then,
rain babies are born –
released to the greening nursery of the world,
with the pitter-patter
of their tiny feet.

Trees
Time spent amongst trees is never wasted time.
– Katrina Mayer

I have an ardor
for an arbor.
All trees are my favorites –
the ones that flower in the Spring,
the ones that riot in the Fall,
the ones, who bare-limbed,
brave Winter's cold and ice, and
the ones who bend and twist in their dance
with the winds at cliff's edge.
But the tree that means the most to me is
the Poet-Tree,
for it offers hope, healing, beauty and solace –
for it is lush,
and evergreen.

Willows

My mother wrote a poem once
in which she described
the willows growing nearby along the river
as having the color of a harlot's hair.
Not at all politically correct
but so accurate –
the brassy orange/red before the greenery appears.
There is a stand of willows
along the bank of a pond I pass by often,
and each time I do,
I think of that line,
and her, my mother,
gone now 40+ years.

Red Rock Canyon

The canyon walls in shade
are chocolate brown,
but where the sun
tips the jutting corners
it becomes, once again,
Red Rock Canyon.

If I sat here for days
I would never feel satisfied
that I had gazed upon
all the colors possible
in this timeless, open-aired chamber,
this rock testimony to change.

I think of Nelson Bentley's quote:
*"The beauty of all forms
is that they take the unchangeable
and express it through the changing."*
Here, now
I know it in my aging bones,
and see it with my fading eyes.

Lilac City Promise

*"A city becomes a world when one
loves one of its inhabitants."*
 – Lawrence Durrell

A Seattle restaurant posts this sign:

*"We reserve the right to serve only
those in love,
those who have been in love,
or those who want to be in love,"*

and I want Spokane to adopt this idea
as a Lilac City promise.
If you don't already have loved ones around,
or even if you do,
pick someone out at the STA plaza –
the single mom struggling with child and stroller,
the older couple standing in line at the Bing,
or ahead of you, the teen with the tatts
at the Knitting Factory.
Love them. Love them all.
Look the homeless man in the eye,
greet him as a neighbor.
Send each one an out-of-season
but continually welcome,
Valentine of compassion.

Just what could this world be coming to?

A Declaration

We are shattered bits of light
broken loose upon the universe.
Remember this during the dark hours
and in reflection.
Have conversations with the stones and stars.
Know that the moon is a patient listener –
as is the Sequoia and the Oak –whose branches lift
and dance with the winds, and whose roots
gnarled and curious, always seek true nourishment.
Be not distracted from your own light,
nor hide it under a bushel. The world is dark enough
and needs your candle flicker.
Laugh with the babbling brook,
and weep with the willow,
cast no shadow aside, for each has something to teach.
Know when to lift your burden, and when to let it rest.
Offer yourself over and over like water tumbling down
a waterfall – that is how love cascades.
Practice joy giving like a songbird each morning,
and whisper a thank you to the night each evening.
And so will your life be a blessing.
Live it!

Moon, Clouds, Trees

I love the accomplishment of the moon,
how she peers as unblinking witness
to the truth;
how she hears whispered confessions
and prayers, yet never spills her secrets.
I love how she alters, but remains herself,
and how she bathes us all in beauty,
cleansing us with moonlight.

I love the playfulness of clouds,
how they skip and dance, and float across the sky,
offering a screen for imagination's projection –
the marquee changing moment to moment.
World travelers with no luggage, they
speak the international language of hope,
as everyone has to look up to see them.

And I love the solidness of trees,
how they offer their shapes as shade,
their lacy silhouettes as comfort.
I love how they dance with the wind,
and quibble with the breeze.
I love that they stand still long enough
to be hugged. They stand tall
to hold up the sky.

Fleeting Magic

I was on a writer's retreat in northern Minnesota
when I encountered my first fireflies,
It was, as countless folks have said, *magical*.
Their flashing seemed random –
maybe they were writing poems in the air?
Later I learned that males and females
each have their own flash pattern –
a call and response conversation in light.
Many years later a friend wrote about her experience
of flying with a glass jar of fireflies
tucked between her knees.
They did not survive long
in her dry eastern Washington garden.
She watched as the flash & response pattern
slowly diminished
until there was only the lone firefly
flashing into the evening,
that no one answered.

Aflutter

Imagine
the breath
as a butterfly
flitting between
the outside and the in
pausing on the threshold
of the lips
to quiver
in exquisite beauty.
Breathing deeply
summons a swarm
of wings
to assemble
in a bouquet
of light and air,
to dive deep within
and dance and spread
through every pathway
filling each muscle and pore
with nourishing light.
With every breath
the butterflies illuminate.
Remember this when
you have to catch your breath –
you are netting butterflies,
and releasing them
into the air
to then be caught
and released
through another's lips.
We are all
aswirl in butterflies.

Love's Staircase

Love's stairs
ascend to hope
and descend
to deeper understanding.

Love's stairs
wind round & round –
either way
you get where you are going.

Love's stairs
have a handrail
to guide the searching heart.
All you need is to hold on
and then,
to let go.

Unmoored

The most difficult conversation
does not take place.

He does not say goodbye.
She does not whisper farewell.

No. Silently, they watch
the boat of their marriage drift
across the lake of years.

He wants harbor somewhere
where she does not.
She wants new sails
while he plunges into cold water
chained to the anchor.

Their children grow up,
jump ship, set their own sails,
while the couple
buoy themselves with outdated life vests –
trying to remember who they are
and who they married.

The oar locks creak and moan
the only accompaniment to silenced
yearnings and dying hopes.

One heads to the sunset.
One heads for the sunrise.
The only music, silence

In Fields of Gold

The vintage enamel coffee pot
sits on my kitchen table
its lid hinged back,
its throat open
like a bird's beak
about to burst forth in song.
Inside, five gorgeous sunflowers
their weighted heads bowed,
yet cheerful, silently sing.
I think of the painter, Van Gogh,
how leaden he must have felt,
amidst all this golden glory
to end his life in a field
of these shining suns,
blinding in their beauty.
Their petals – golden tongues
whispering the names of God.

Out of Darkness

*"darkness which holds us in its loose pocket all night
sets us down..."*
 – Naomi Shihab Nye

I wouldn't mind being
inside darkness' pocket
if it meant I was jingling about
with the loose change of stars,
colliding with moonlight's shiny quarter.

Perhaps that's the magic
of sleep, where night is
as deep as the ocean
and diving into that pocket
we net our dreams –
slippery as fishes,
flashing their silver
like coins,
and we are changed,
and change alike.

At daybreak, night turns
his pockets inside out
and pulls up one gold coin,
and you wonder,
how did you spend your night?

Between the Sheets

The body's cursive
lies between the sheets
as sleep writes the dreamer's sentences
in a language of image and cryptic metaphor.
Someone once said that a dream
is an unopened letter to oneself.
In daylight, we try to decipher
the handwriting
written in moonlight's invisible ink.
And to answer it,
with our lives.

Haiku on Sleep

sleep's magic kingdom
transforms a crabby person
into an angel

slipping inside sheets
my bed an envelope
mailed to dreamland

Dreams

Dreams do come
and dreams do call.
Listen, listen
with your all:

A whisper,
a fragment,
a dissolving scene,
a shadowy figure
what does it mean?

A person,
an image,
a wild, wild beast,
a finding, a feeling,
a secret unleashed.

A spilling,
a sifting,
a smoky milieu,
the dreams they are calling,
calling to you.

A searching,
a seeking,
a time to review,
a secret to treasure
is locked within you.

Remember,
remember,
to hold to the light
the mysterious messages
of the dark night.

Looking Glass World

Dreams are always peopled.
Some you know, or think you do,
and others who are strangers in a strange land.
Where can you go for solitude in a dream?
You might walk along a shore,
or enter a dark wood – but soon
all is animated. The ocean roars,
the trees speak with the tongues of their leaves.
Dreams are not still-lifes hung in this nighttime gallery.
Wandering hallways that may dissolve,
turning down corridors interrupted by corners,
you follow some unknown path, eyeing everything.
Finally, you encounter a painting, a portrait.
You lean in, look closer.
A face you almost recognize?
It keeps changing.
Is it a mirror?
Study it.

Twilight Zone

A counselor once told me
that a person with schizophrenia
cannot tell reality from dream,
and dream from reality.

To be lost like that
in a personal and private
twilight zone, unable to escape
the mists, is tragic.

We now live in a political time
where fake news
and outlandish notions
have overtaken reason
and spread, unchecked.

Too many have let
their anger and fear
animate their absurd reality
to which they cannot even
be shaken awake.

And this is a nightmare,
not a dream.
Oh where is Rod Serling
when you need him?

Empty Corridor

The empty corridor
only feels lonely
when the tap
of footsteps
recedes.

The stage,
empty of actors,
seems to hold
its breath
until the door
of the green room
opens.

The garage awaits
the car
like a shoebox
awaiting the shoe,
bereft, until it slips
right in.

The magician's top hat
black as night
becomes blacker
once the white rabbit
escapes.

My heart,
an acrobat of pulse
and tumble
prefers soliloquy
to circus.

Rabbit Moon

for JMS

Last night I awoke
thinking of you, my first love,
long ago untethered
except for that small green tendril
named friendship.
In my dream, you were a white rabbit
nibbling on the half-buried cabbage of my heart,
your whiskers quivering.
I only saw the beauty of white rabbit in moonlight.

Forty years ago
under moonlit skies we walked
and talked through empty Missoula streets –
you philosophizing on the meaning of life,
I sharing my dreams.
Yesterday I found your letters tucked in a box
in my closet, half–buried in out-of-season stuff
the remains of your distancing and betrayal.

I think of burning them, or tossing them away,
but my harbored loyalty
to the young man you once were
makes me think of sending them all back to you.
Perhaps you'll read them under moonlit skies
and the thought of me
will nibble at the cabbage of your heart.

The Bus of Questions

Oh save me a seat on the bus of questions
As we curve around the Mystery asking why?
Oh save me a seat on the bus of questions
As we circle 'round the center once again.

I want a window seat,
You take the aisle.
Isn't it amazing we've gone another mile?
There isn't any road map,
There isn't any plan,
There isn't any schedule
Meeting where I am.

The roads they have no street lamps,
The signs are not one way.
With detours we meander,
At construction we delay.

Zigging to the left now –
Zagging to the right,
I guess we're making progress,
It's hard to tell at night.

Are we going 'round in circles?
Or are we going around the bend?
Are we coming to forever?
Are we coming to the end?

Oh, our baggage is encumbering,
Our luggage is not light.
It's packed with dreams and terror,
Folded all up tight.
Oh our clothes all are wrinkled,
There are creases in our souls.
The grime and dust of travel
Color what we know.

Am I getting lost again?
Or am I being found?
I keep going on and on
And round and round.
Are you getting carsick?
Or are you getting well?
It's not on any timetable
It's really hard to tell.

Oh save me a seat on the bus of questions
As we wonder round and round.
What is our destination?
Why is it so profound?
What is the path we travel?
What is the path we roam?
Wherever it is going –
It is a place called home.

Lemon

A slice of lemon,
so simple.

A bit of golden heaven,
so simple.

A wheel of pulp
so simple.

A disc of sunlight,
so simple.

A womb of seeds,
so simple.

A divinity of delight,
so simple.

A blessing of juice,
so simple.

A humdinger
of sour,

but still,
simply
perfection.

Skinny Dip

Isn't it remarkable
how the magic of touch
can tame or ignite?

Our skin, so receptive,
is the conduit
to caution or cheer.

All the while calling us
to be mindful
for whatever signal is present.

Blue Dog

Depression, like a dog
follows me everywhere,
nipping at my heels.
I must stop and pet
my companion.
"Heel," I say.
"Heal."

Invisible Enemy

My depression bares down on me
making it hard to function.
It is like having an invisible enemy –
you can't see it, but evidence
abounds in messiness and disorganization.
It robs me of motivation and energy.
Occasionally I'll have a glimpse
of the old Lisa, and I'll remember
how I used to feel,
until that dark shadow embraces me
in a bear hug, once again.
I am struggling to recover,
to have those glimpses of my old self
last longer and longer until
it is my depressed self that is gone, dismissed, lost.
My mother was hospitalized with a schizophrenia diagnosis,
manifesting in deep depression.
She was a writer – a journalist and poet,
and for a long time I associated her creativity
with madness, and I feared falling into the same pit.
But poetry offers me a ladder to climb out of it,
and slowly, very slowly, rung by rung,
I am lifting myself out.

Wherefore Art Thou, Peace?

Bombs and blood,
dust and rubble –
destruction all around
in country, region, or territory.
We never learn.
No one ever wins in war –
just the munitions makers
and arms manufacturers.
May their sleep be troubled
with nightmares
of what their work has wrought.
May they realize that their nightmares
are others' reality.
May they just stop.
The green of profit
is no fitting match for the red of blood
spilled over imaginary boundaries,
or differing religious belief.
No victory is lasting.
Our flaw as humans is to
think our way is the best and only right one,
while unaware or ignorant
of other ways from differing folk.
Fear is our flaw,
but efforts to understand and empathize,
our greatest gift.
Let us all, be brave, and use it.

Full Moon

The full moon gazes down
on my father's dead face
I kiss him goodbye on his forehead,
smoothed now,
as he enters a new phase.
The Virginia cicadas chirp
their chorus of forget-me-nots.
In the kitchen, the ripened mango
waits while we say goodbye
for the last time.

Friend's Bedside

for Darlene Melvin

At my friend's bedside
we talk of gardens,
and poem-writing,
and the beautiful color
of eggplants.
I lift her small dog,
Li-Po, named after the Chinese poet
to her side. They both drift
in the duet of petting and sighing.
His fur is warm from the sun
he has been soaking up
on the front porch
before I let him back in.
She looks out at her front garden
and the soft sculpture of snow melting
on this blue and white
beautiful day.
I read to her from Thich Nhat Hanh
who speaks of mindfully washing vegetables.
We share a quiet moment
knowing it is not just the eggplant
that is a jewel,
but our being alive together
in this moment,
breathing in and out,
the dog asleep at her side.

The Eye

The eyeball of the television
blinks out at midnight,
following the Air Force Anthem –
Off we go into the wild blue yonder.
Then the test pattern
resembling an Indian Head penny
in a circle target comes on.
Only 3 channels then,
everything black and white.
The eyeball's retina watched
hundreds of westerns, cartoons and dramas,
heard hundreds of laugh tracks,
and occasionally was snow-bound
for indeterminate times.
It watched as major events unfolded –
tragedies like the Kennedy assassination,
and triumphs like men walking on the moon.
It stared at us,
the faces in the room,
while we stared at it –
mesmerized by its flickering images
as if it were a modern version of a campfire –
captivating us with stories.

In the Air

The salty air
is sweet,
for someone
who has long been away
from the sea.

Breathing the air
once again,
it seems my heart,
as well as my lungs,
are filled.

Memories of other
beach visits come.
The surf, the waves, the tide
are ever changing,
but reliably the same.

Yes, this salty air,
is sweet.

I'm Sorry

I'm sorry this sounds lame –
I was up too late drinking
coffee. Or was it absinthe?
I am so absent-minded!
I was on my way to
class, but got caught red-handed –
even though I'm really blue–
(this is an election year after all)
writing jokes
that don't stand up
late night
or otherwise,
But I was cruising when
a poetry speed bump
made me halt
to look at the moon
and then the honking I heard behind me
was not Canadian geese
but the horns of plenty
honk, honk, honking
on heaven's door –
which is where my mind
wandered
thinking of you
peering over heaven's gate –
the one with the squeaky hinge.
And
all I know is that
it swings wide open
like my heart does,
the way poetry does for me.

Poetry pouring its sweetness like sugar,
and sifting the salt, like tears
sifting, sifting,
shifting gears now – I pull over for poetry.
My bumper sticker states, *"I brake for haiku."*
You'll find me parked now –
my steering wheel rotating round
my thoughts, wheeling –
musing around corners and steering through stanzas.
I stop for deadlines,
but sometimes I roll right through.
Want a ride?

Dear Snoopy

Dear Snoopy,

You are my comic super-hero,
flying by the seat of your pants
(if you had any)
up there, on top of that doghouse —
tapping away clickety-clack
on your Royal Underwood —
diving and soaring with
your imagination unfettered
by leash or license.
You are as bold as the WWI flying ace
you bark about.
Oh Snoopy,
if only I could
order up some room service —
supper in a dish
to my airy studio in the clouds,
where I'd skillfully
tap dance on my computer
right past
<u>it was a dark and stormy night</u>
into literary fame,
where I'd call you up and make a date
to see you in the funny papers.

Centaur & Griffin

On occasion, I will succumb
to a fervent poetic trance,
unaware of anything
except my imagination,
which can be a bit quirky
and does not follow
a logical script.
So a centaur may guard the elevator
waiting for his friend, the griffin –
a symbol of divine power
and heavenly protection, to arrive –
but with his wings, why take the elevator?
But that's the way of these imaginary adventures –
nonsensical, fickle and sometimes, risque,
but which are an antidote to the ordinary,
tepid business of living.
I try not be peevish,
but sometimes I can't help it.
I would like to wholeheartedly
celebrate my imagination –
giving it a deserving ovation,
especially during these troubled times.

Unlikely Pair

Barbie lifts her shirt
and shows her hard plastic boobs.
Raggedy Ann blushes as she
lifts her dress
to show her heart tattoo,
"I LOVE YOU" in block letters.
Barbie is clearly annoyed,
she's always at the gym
or the beauty salon
or on the runway
holding her legs and arms
stiffly, flailing,
trying to attract attention
from the glitterati & the paparazzi.
Raggedy Ann, however, just sighs.
She's content
plopped on a bed or pillow.
A home-body, she prefers
vintage clothing -
floral dress, striped stockings, old-fashioned apron.
Raggedy Ann, such a good listener,
asks Barbie, "Would you like me to fix you something?
Milk & cookies?"
Barbie turns her cosmetically correct head,
and stares at R.A.

"My figure won't allow it." she declares,
even though Raggedy Ann can hear
Barbie's tiny stomach growl.
Raggedy Ann's button eyes fill with unspilled tears.
She knows how lonely Barbie must be.
Ken is no stellar boyfriend.
He'd rather play war games than house,
and is often away rolling in the dirt
with G.I. Joe.
Raggedy Ann shares the bed with Teddy Bear,
often waking up with her arms around him.
His fur is ticklish.
Conversation between these dolls is strained and shallow.
Barbie doesn't think about much,
except about how she looks.
In the end, Raggedy Ann offers to comb Barbie's hair
and put it up in a fancy "do."
She laughs a hearty laugh, not minding at all
that her own bed-headed hair is just a tangled ball
of red yarn.

Metamorphosis

The sporty convertible
darts in and out of traffic
like a hummingbird.
Its green color
shimmering iridescent
in the sun.
Then a cherry red
vintage VW approaches,
reminiscent of a ladybug
flying her way home.
And a truck's lost retread –
called an alligator
for its resemblance
to that creature –
lies curled on the side of the road.
Inanimate things
suddenly alive and enormous –
what if these imaginative
fleets of fancy come true?
Would it be a fantastical dream,
or a nightmare?
Only the dreamer knows.

At Walden Pond

Beware of all enterprises that require new clothes,
Thoreau wrote, in his advocation of the simple life.
Ironic, since he lived *"self-reliantly"*
in a 10 x15 foot cabin at Walden Pond,
but his mother did his laundry.

God's Purse

At the bottom
of God's purse,
is
change.

After the Vows

Cinderella's pumpkin carriage
turned into a two-seater convertible.
Prince Charming
commanded the wheel
wearing leather driving gloves
and sporting a mustache
like a caterpillar.
She had to squeeze in
beside his golf clubs.
Cinderella was not any
too keen to play golf–
especially in slick glass slippers.
She wanted desperately to go dancing.
But now the muddy,
rutted road ahead, and
dark storm clouds
would keep her from the ballroom –
not to mention her Prince's
preoccupation with the green.
Wary of grass stains
and a water logged gown,
plus the prospect
of a dull and boring honeymoon,
Cinderella throttled
the car,
or was it the Prince?

Fantasy Want Ads

For Sale: Used Coach
Pumpkin-colored, low mileage
(Once around the kingdom)
Enchanted bill of sale
Must sell before midnight!!!

Property for Sale:
Charming cottage on Tiger Lilly Cove
In Never Never Land
Must release, owner about to grow up
Contact TinkerBell Reality at 777-7777

For Rent:
Oddly shaped house with many bedrooms
just off Shoe Leather Lane

Dorothy's Day Care:
Openings
for munchkins of all ages
Located on yellow-brick road, Oz

Lost:
One great White Whale
please text me at Ishmael.com

Found:
One large Golden Egg,
believed to be recently laid,
White goose feather attached
To Claim:
Come in person to Newspaper Office

To Flirt

In a different time,
a lady would show
her interest, or lack thereof
with a flick of her wrist,
her fan, a kind of banner
proclaiming indirectly
her emotional state, her feeling
for the apparent suitor.
Sometimes I wish
we could rewind back
to that old-fashioned time
that seems more simple
than our own.
OMG
LOL
EMOJI, EMOJI, EMOJI

Umbrellas

Umbrellas twirl
in carnival colors sprouting
against the asphalt ground, while
the flowering trees toss their petals
like confetti onto the streets and driveways.
If it's raining on my parade, I really don't
mind
all this
l
u
s
c
i
o
u
s
ness.

Postal Script

Sitting down to write
is akin to opening the mailbox –
there is an element of possibility
and expectant hope.
Will I get a letter from a friend?

Will I find the just right words
in just the right order?

Will my mail be all bills?

Will I stub my pencil on a writer's block?

Will I get a landslide of appeals
for worthy causes –
save the whales, the elephants, the donkeys
forcing me to catch my breath
and drop them in the recycling bin,
even though I am aligned with,
or in favor of each of their causes?.
I can't send dollars to everyone who asks.

Will I run out of ideas?
Out of ink? Out of time?
Will I make too many false starts?
I can't follow every lead or idea,
no matter how worthy.
Will I need to drop my ideas completely,
or recycle them with adjustment or revision?

What the mailbox and the paper & pen
have in common, is hope, potential,
in the spaciousness of the empty mailbox,
and of the blank page.
I have to reach inside the mailbox,
I have to reach inside myself.

Loss

Little by little
memories fade
and body parts wear.

But broken down
may just as easily be
broken open.

Our losses expose
vulnerabilities and fragilities
and our own mortality.

Losses also awaken us
to what we cherish, what matters,
and in that loss, we gain.

Poem Prayer

for all the missing indigenous women
in North America

The young woman,
the teenager,
the sister,
the cousin,
the single mom, struggling,
are missing from our circle.
Where have they disappeared to?

May the grasses and the trees,
the mountains, rivers, and streams
accompany and comfort them
wherever they may be,
under the stars –
even if their voices now
are only whispered by the wind.

The Meaning of Life

No one I ask knows
the meaning of life.
They respond with nervous giggles
or furrowed brows,
some with just a shrug.
Others take it as an invitation
to pontificate
or evangelize.
Occasionally someone will return the question,
and I answer:

I am passing through
this life
as we each are.
Ignorant of so much
yet cognizant (hopefully)
of the beauty around me.
This is my truth.

Around the dinner table
I ask the question again
and someone is afraid to answer,
or cannot answer,
and then a small voice
from a small child
pipes up,
"to love, silly!"

Smiles beam around the table
and we are all
a little wiser
and more grateful,
than ever before.

Golden Hour

In medicine, the golden hour
is the first few minutes
when treatment
surges healing forward.
In photography, the golden hour
is those last fleeting moments
of the setting sun
whose rays glaze the landscape
with a rich and ambered luster.
Each of these times are marked
with the urgency of immediacy.
But for me, the golden hour
are those moments
when time's swift foot
ambles instead,
lingering among the honeyed layers
of sweet understanding,
until the nugget of
love's radiance
reveals its simple glory.

For Len
for Leonard Pung

You have suddenly slipped
from your moorings
and gone out into the vastness
of the unknown,
the last great adventure.
But still
your light lingers here
in our hearts.
I remember a brown-eyed boy
with book in hand,
and a punster extraordinaire
with your arched eyebrow and bemused grin.
Fueled on caffeine
and determined enthusiasm
you struck deep into the heart
of your writing dream,
chiseling and polishing
line by line
the worlds you created.
Having overcome self-doubt,
a roomful of middle-schoolers,
you worked your recovery
and set a new course.
Just on the brink of perfecting your craft
you rode the rapids of your last river,
and too soon,
too soon,
you left us.
The waters rise now in our grief
and lift you up
in our love.

In the Folds of Mystery
for Darlene Melvin

As my friend gently
leaves this world,
I am reminded
of all my deep losses –
my mother,
my brother,
my friend,
and I mourn them
anew.

The pain of their leaving
tears my horizon open
like a sun,
setting.

Such beauty
is fading into mystery
where I cannot go
yet, but when I do,
I will join all
my loved ones
in the folds of that mystery,
and we will be
one.

Awakening

for Kitty Eagle

"Your vision will come clear only
when you look inside your heart.
Who looks outside dreams.
Who looks inside, awakens."
  - Carl Jung

My sister-in-law died yesterday morning.
She lived a good life, but it was cut short at 69.
Her dream was singing. She had a beautiful voice.
Her brain tumor robbed her of her singing,
then her speaking,
her understanding,
herself,
but, turning inward
as she did towards the end –
closing down the outside,
I'd like to think that she was awakening to
what matters most –
her soul, and her faith that sustained her
for a journey into a heavenly choir.

A Simple Request

All my dying friend
wished for, near the end,
was the taste
of pineapple juice
on her tongue.

Such a simple request,
but it contained
the world.

It still breaks
my heart
when I think of it.

Dying

dying is a labor
and we, inexperienced midwives
last breath as precious as first

in death's waiting room
a single flower blooms
pointing to heaven

caregivers worn out
of everything
but love

A Softer Landing

We have been gifted by the lives
of those who have passed and gone before us.

The weight of their loss
aches within us, large and looming.

But as we think of them,
we are lifted by remembrances
of their qualities and quirks,
their ideals and idiosyncrasies,
their passions and persuasions,
their features, even their flaws.

We remember meaningful conversations
and lively discussions,
moments of laughter,
or of beauty, shared.

May we remember those times cooking together,
hiking or volunteering,
of concerts celebrated and songs sung,
or just the quiet sharing of hopes, fears and dreams,
around a table.

May we remember what they loved –
their families, friends, pets, gardens, nature.

And may we remember them
through the light of our love,
which illuminates and expands their lives
beyond their absent breathing,
and gives us a softer landing in our sorrow.

A Musing on Angels

I don't know whether I believe in angels.
I don't know even if I want to believe in angels.
No matter how benevolent–
Do I want someone always watching, staring at me?
Even watching over me implies an immense
disenfranchisement of power.

And anyway, wouldn't any angel
watching over me be bored
with my quiet, poetic life?
There'd be much more excitement
and thrill somewhere else, I'm sure –
worthy even, of feather-plucking worry.

If I had an angel, I'd imagine him as muse,
watching clouds, not resting on them.
His poet heart would hum along with the bees in summer,
his sorrow float like flakes of snow in winter,
coating the world in gauze.
He would question everything, and know no answers.

Perhaps he would play a harmonica instead of a harp,
and he'd whisper riddles into my ear like
the wind whispers in the leaves.
He'd hold my longing like a Valentine
and comfort me with touches of kindness.

I don't know how much flying he would do
with his burdensome appendages,
but maybe he'd kiss the words in my poems
and make them soar
on borrowed wings.

Tandem

"A boundary is not that at which something stops,
but that from which something begins."
– Martin Heidegger

A threshold is both
a doorway
and a boundary.
Like sunrise
is the opening of the day,
and also,
the demise of night.

But we dwell on morning,
hardly giving a thought to
the departing night
who leaves the scarlet cloak of dawn
disheveled on horizon's floor.

At My Memorial

Suppose,
just suppose
like a hood ornament bird
set free at last
to soar, unfettered,
I should decide to perch
on a shoulder,
your shoulder, say
while you are attending
my memorial service.
Would you be able to identify me?
My small metallic weight
tickling your ear,
whispering irreverent thoughts
or silly jokes –
anything to ease the viscosity of grief
of your missing me
(I hope)
Why a metallic bird
not some ethereally winged
angel messenger?
Why, don't you know,
I have a tin ear
but now at last
I can sing to my heart's content
and all you will hear
will be sweet nothings.

Acknowledgements

To poet, Dennis Held, who initially looked over my poems and gave me good suggestions and recommendations regarding publication.

To poet and publisher, Edmond Bruneau, for his loving friendship and encouragement during this process of getting into print. I couldn't have done it without him.

To Donna Lange, for her eye for edit and detail.

To Rhea Giffin, whose friendship and invitation to share a studio, birthed so much creativity in art and poetry.

To Kelly LaGrutta & Peggy Eklof for setting **"The Bus of Questions,"** *to music and singing it in their group,* **"Planted by Hand."**

To poet, C.L. Crowell, my sweetheart, for his loving support and care.

To Annica Eagle & Emily Eagle, for their technical know-how, and their love.

Inspirations

Aflutter after *Little Champion* by Tony Hoagland.

Apples of Memory after *Truant* by Margaret Hasse.

At My Memorial after *Driving Myself to a Poetry Reading* by Billy Collins.

Beneath Our Star after *Nothing Twice* by Wislawa Szymborska.

Between the Sheets after *The Blue Blanket* by Sue Ellen Thomson.

Calendar Suite from a line from *Today* by William Stafford.

How Hard It Is To Be Outgrown after *Mother Talks Back to the Monster* by Connie Shippers.

Leaning Forward after *Places of Meaning* by William Stafford.

Life Is Short after *Good Bones* by Maggie Smith.

Not Afraid of the Dark from *Words When We Need Them* by Naomi Shihab Nye.

Moon, Clouds, Trees after *A Final Affection* by Paul Zimmer.

Poet's Song after *Samurai Song* by Robert Pinsky.

The Poet Looks at Her Own Work after *A Lobsterman Looks at The Sea* by Dr. Richard Berlin.

Where I'm From template by George Ella Lyons.

Wonder-Full after *The Journey* by David Whyte.

Publication Histories

A Softer Landing was commissioned by the
UU Church of Spokane for their annual Requiem Service

Dreams was painted on a papier-mâché art piece circa 2000

Fantasy Want Ads appeared in the **Cheney Free Press**,
11/11/21

God's Purse appeared in the Fall 2005 **UU World Magazine**,
and was painted on a papier-mâché art piece

I'm Sorry appeared in **Spokewrite**, 2008

Lilac City Promise appeared in the **Spokesman Review,**
6/8/18

Metamorphosis appeared in the **Cheney Free Press**, 8/21/21

Surprise! appeared in the **Cheney Free Press**, 4/28/22

The Bus of Questions was part of a collaborative art piece
in the exhibit, *"Telling the American Story,"* as part of the
Get Lit Festival, 2011

Vessel appeared in the **Cheney Free Press**, 8/31/23

Unmoored & *Working Fire* appeared in **The Poetry Diner,
or How Not to Order Eggs**, copyrighted by the 2010 Corbin
Senior Center Poetry Class

Why I Write/Why I Don't Write appeared in the **Society
for Childrens' Writers & Book Illustrators** newsletter

www.ingramcontent.com/pod-product-compliance
Lightning Source LLC
Chambersburg PA
CBHW041930090426
42744CB00016B/1995